If you were a
Plural Word

by Trisha Speed Shaskan
illustrated by Sara Gray

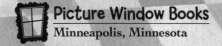

Picture Window Books
Minneapolis, Minnesota

plural word a word that shows more than one person, place, or thing

Editor: Jill Kalz
Designer: Abbey Fitzgerald
Page Production: Melissa Kes
Art Director: Nathan Gassman
Editorial Director: Nick Healy
Creative Director: Joe Ewest
The illustrations in this book were created with acrylics.

Picture Window Books
1710 Roe Crest Drive
North Mankato, MN 56003
www.capstonepub.com

Special thanks to our advisers for their expertise:

Rosemary G. Palmer, Ph.D., Literacy Consultant

Terry Flaherty, Ph.D., Professor of English
Minnesota State University, Mankato

Library of Congress Cataloging-in-Publication Data
Shaskan, Trisha Speed, 1973-
If you were a plural word / by Trisha Speed Shaskan ;
illustrated by Sara Gray.
p. cm. — (Word fun)
Includes index.
ISBN 978-1-4048-5516-8 (library binding)
ISBN 978-1-4048-5696-7 (paperback)
1. English language—Noun—Juvenile literature.
2. English language—Number—Juvenile literature.
I. Gray, Sara, ill. II. Title.
PE1216.S53 2009
428.1—dc22   2009002707

If you were a plural word ...

... you would never be alone.

cow (singular)

cows (plural)

If you were a plural word, you would be more than one person, place, or thing. You could be a singular noun plus the letter s.

One **snake** pushes a **block**.
Three **snakes** push three **blocks**.

One **camel** watches, while the other **camels** lift the blocks.

7

If you were a plural word, you could be a noun plus the letters *es*. When nouns end in *ch, s, sh, x,* or *z,* they become plural by adding *es*.

The **witch** shows her class how to make a dress. She wraps the finished dress in a **box**.

After the **witch_es_** sew their dress_es_, they put them in **box_es_**.

If you were a noun that ends with a vowel and the letter y, you would become plural by adding s.

Larry's **key** opens the big box. Fred's **keys** open the little boxes.

One **tray** isn't big enough to hold the treasure.
So Mimi uses two **tray<u>s</u>**.

If you were a noun that ends with a consonant and the letter y, you would become plural by changing the y to i and adding es.

The **puppy** invites his friends and **family** to a birthday party. A fly thinks she is invited, too.

12

Many **puppies** and their **families** show up. So do lots of **flies!**

If you were a noun that ends with a consonant and the letter o, you would become plural by adding *s* or *es*. Nouns ending with a vowel before the o, such as *video*, always add *s* (*videos*).

A **hippo** and a **rhino** make **tomato** sandwiches for everyone at the picnic.

But the other **hippos** and **rhinos** don't like **tomatoes**.

15

If you were a noun that ends with the letters *f* or *fe*, you would become plural by changing the *f* or *fe* to *v* and adding *es*.

The **elf** and his **wife** bake a **loaf** of raisin bread.

The **elves** and their **wives** make the tastiest **loaves** in town!

bread

If you were a plural word, you could be made by breaking the rules.

A child becomes children.

A goose becomes geese.

A mouse becomes mice.

A woman becomes women.

A person becomes people.

19

If you were a plural word, you could even look exactly the same as your singular form.

A deer, a sheep, and a moose have a hat party.

The **deer** wear baseball caps.

The **sheep** wear pink, feathered hats.

The **moose** wear cowboy hats.

If you were a plural word ...

... you would always be **more** than **one**.

CREATING PLURAL WORDS

Copy the following words on a sheet of paper. Write the plural word next to each singular word. You may want to look back through the book to remember all the rules for changing singular nouns to plural nouns. Check your answers on the next page.

What you need:

a sheet of paper
a pen or pencil

pig	woman	mess
apple	half	bench
potato	pizza	studio
belly	baseball	wolf
watch	fox	goose

Glossary

consonant—a letter of the alphabet other than a, e, i, o, or u (sometimes y)

noun—a word that names a person, place, or thing

plural—more than one

singular—just one

vowel—one of the following letters of the alphabet: a, e, i, o, or u (sometimes y)

To Learn More

More Books to Read

Heinrichs, Ann. *Nouns*. Chanhassen, Minn.: Child's World, 2004.

Pulver, Robin. *Nouns and Verbs Have a Field Day*. New York: Holiday House, 2006.

Internet Sites

FactHound offers a safe, fun way to find Internet sites related to this book. All of the sites on FactHound have been researched by our staff.

Here's all you do:

Visit www.facthound.com

FactHound will fetch the best sites for you!

Look for all of the books in the Word Fun series:

If You Were a Capital Letter
If You Were a Comma
If You Were a Compound Word
If You Were a Conjunction
If You Were a Contraction
If You Were a Homonym or a Homophone
If You Were a Noun
If You Were a Palindrome
If You Were a Period
If You Were a Plural Word
If You Were a Prefix
If You Were a Preposition
If You Were a Pronoun
If You Were a Question Mark
If You Were a Suffix
If You Were a Synonym
If You Were a Verb
If You Were Alliteration
If You Were an Adjective
If You Were an Adverb
If You Were an Antonym
If You Were an Apostrophe
If You Were an Exclamation Point
If You Were an Interjection
If You Were Onomatopoeia
If You Were Quotation Marks

Answers from page 23

pig / pigs	woman / women	mess / messes
apple / apples	half / halves	bench / benches
potato / potatoes	pizza / pizzas	studio / studios
belly / bellies	baseball / baseballs	wolf / wolves
watch / watches	fox / foxes	goose / geese